Dedication

To my lovely wife, JonNisha, and to my son Ellery, who help me breathe easy.

Also

Thank YOU for investing your time and money into this book. I hope the concepts benefit you as much as they have benefited me.

Don't Forget To Breathe

Inhale Opportunities & Exhale Results

By Dauv Evans, Ph.D.

Don't Forget To Breathe

Inhale Opportunities & Exhale Results

By Dauv Evans, Ph.D.

ISBN-10:0615937861
ISBN-13:9780615937861

For additional information please visit: www.dauvevans.com

Table of Contents

Introduction

Anyone who knows me can tell you that I am a documentary junkie. Documentaries are the perfect combination of my two favorite things, movies and learning. Years ago, I watched a series of documentaries all in one weekend - I was in heaven. The people who were the focus of the documentaries were from all over the world and were renowned for very different endeavors: Mahatma Gandhi, Amelia Earhart, Bill Gates, Earvin "Magic" Johnson, Warren Buffett, and Martin Luther King Jr.

In the back of my mind I felt like there must be commonality they all shared, but I couldn't quite put my finger on it. A few days went by before it hit me: these people's success was not a characteristic of specific tasks they had performed; rather, it was a way of life for them. Everything they touched, people they met, places they went were all potential opportunities.

For example, would you consider Warren Buffett to be successful? He is one of the wealthiest men in the world, but that is not what stuck out to me about him. Buffett is known for identifying opportunities that seemed to be hidden to others. For example, he's been known to invest in financially unattractive businesses and turn a profit. Buffett faced challenges early in his career. He was unable to find employment on Wall Street right after graduate school which was one of his goals. He also was not great with communicating with others which hindered him from making the connections he needed to work on Wall Street.

Buffett was able to overcome both of these issues by working as a stockbroker in his hometown of Omaha, Nebraska. He became more proficient with his communication skills after enrolling in Dale Carnegie's course: *How to Win Friends & Influence People.*

Buffett eventually started his own partnership in Omaha. The first five years Buffett was in business the DOW went up by 74%, but his investments had gone up by 250% and became a millionaire by age 30. He later purchased the fledgling textile mill Berkshire Hathaway.

Buffett purchased the company, extracted the money out of the business, and reinvested it in the insurance business. The textile mill faded away, but he retained the name for his now multibillion-dollar company. He set out to make money in the stock market and business and he did.

Martin Luther King Jr. is another figure I'm sure you're familiar with. Would you consider him to be successful? King was a civil rights activist who fought for equal rights for African Americans in the U.S. He worked with other activist such as Ralph Abernathy, Bayard Rustin, and many others to garner national attention to the issue of civil rights. King faced much opposition. He was jailed, ridiculed, and eventually assassinated for what he believed.

King's aim was to eradicate racism, social injustice, and inequality for African Americans in the U.S. Do racism, social injustice, and inequality still exist today? If King did not eliminate the aforementioned social ails from the U.S. then why do we consider Martin Luther King Jr. a successful person?

Some of the people took ostensibly ordinary situations and transformed them into extraordinary successes. It seemed to me almost as though they breathed success; it seemed that success came as naturally to them as breathing. This realization prompted me to redefine my sense of success and create my mantra, which you'll learn later in this book.

Breathing Success Assessment

Before you begin the book, take a moment to answer these questions as honestly as you can, based upon how you feel right at this moment. Total your score on the next page. We'll review your results later in the reading.

I constantly think about my goals and what it takes to reach them

1 Very Untrue 2 Untrue 3Neutral 4 True 5 Very True

I enjoy meeting new people all the time

1 Very Untrue 2 Untrue 3Neutral 4 True 5 Very True

I get a sense of satisfaction from working toward my goals

1 Very Untrue 2 Untrue 3Neutral 4 True 5 Very True

I like to try new activities when I have the chance

1 Very Untrue 2 Untrue 3Neutral 4 True 5 Very True

Earning a lot of money is not one of my main goals

1 Very Untrue 2 Untrue 3Neutral 4 True 5 Very True

The last time I made progress toward one of my goals was

1 > Month 2 Month - 2 Weeks 3 A Week 4 Yesterday 5 Today

Helping others is more important than obtaining lavish items

1 Very Untrue 2 Untrue 3Neutral 4 True 5 Very True

Regardless of life's obstacles, I never give up on reaching my goals

1 Very Untrue 2 Untrue 3Neutral 4 True 5 Very True

Success in my life is measured by

1 Money 2 My Career 3 Amount of Friends 4 My Lifestyle 5 Other

Total:_____

Chapter 1

Holding Your Breath

"Breathing, according to me, corresponds to taking charge of one's own life." ~ *Luce Irigaray*

Take a deep *breath* as you reflect on where you are in life. Take another deep breath and think about where you want to be in life. Inhale one last time and hold it for five seconds before exhaling and think about what you're willing to do to build the life you want. As you learn more about the breathing success principle ask yourself "how does this apply to my life." Now, let us begin with the end in mind.

What if you could spend the majority of the week doing something you truly enjoy? What if you could change other peoples' lives for the better? Does a two-week vacation at a resort in the Caribbean surrounded by crystal-clear water and white, sandy beaches interest you? Imagine if you had the ability to consistently achieve your goals. Or more importantly, what if you could finally consider yourself "successful?"

Do the aforementioned items resemble anything you've ever wanted in life? If so, have these items seemed to be just out of your reach? Do you feel you are undeserving of these things? Do you think you need to simply work harder in order to attain them?

Maybe you think you lack the means or knowhow to obtain these things. Some may say that acquiring them just depends on luck.

Take another moment to think of one thing you have been able to acquire so far. For example, a grade you received in a course, a promotion you earned, or maybe a product you saved your money to purchase. Do you think that was luck too? No, of course not. You recognized an opportunity, took advantage of it, and were successful in that specific endeavor.

When your mind is fixated on a goal, obstacles are no longer barriers; they simply become a breathing pattern for you to follow as you run this marathon of life. If you take a second to think about it, you do this all the time without even realizing it.

If you attempt to reach any goal that will require a certain amount of energy and resources, you might pace yourself. You'll find some way to track your incremental progress toward your goal.

This automatic process keeps you from depleting your resources too soon and helps you identify the necessary steps required to reach your goal. Some people have a propensity to get frustrated by the idea of obstacles and want to give up before they have even really gotten started, but you do not have to be one of those people.

When you learn how to apply the "breathing success" principle to your life, you will see a significant change in your perspective. You will notice that opportunities are everywhere, like air, and that success can be as natural as the process of breathing.

This book will show you how to find opportunities and get the results you want so that you can be successful in life. If you're already starting to get some ideas about how these concepts might apply to your own life, feel free to use the thought bubble starting on page 96 to jot down your thoughts.

Holding My Breath

Today I am able to say I am doing the things I love for a living: teaching, speaking, and training. My career allows me to live the lifestyle that I want. My career requires me to travel and meet interesting people and change lives for the better. How did I get here, you ask? Well, let me start from the beginning.

The process of getting to where I am today was not easy. I didn't always have the foresight to take advantage of the opportunities around me. I worked in sales at Cingular wireless and Alltel, which both go by different names now, after graduating from the University of North Carolina at Greensboro in 2004. Sales did not interest me; my dream was working in higher education.

My professional career in higher education began as an Academic Advisor at the University of Phoenix (UOPx) in 2006. I still remember searching for jobs almost every day while still working at Alltel until one day I received a phone call one afternoon from someone at UOPx regarding a position as an Enrollment Counselor.

At that point, I had applied to so many jobs that I did not remember applying for this specific position. Although I did not get an offer for the Enrollment Counselor position, they called me in again to interview for another position, Academic Counselor. I was excited because the position would allow me to work with students and get my foot in the door working in higher education.

I initially enjoyed my job. I woke up every day feeling a sense of satisfaction with the work I was doing because I knew I was on the right path. The process of assisting adult students was challenging, but rewarding. The students I worked with were faced with all kinds of challenging situations, but they worked hard to overcome their challenges.

I had a great manager and outgoing coworkers who were encouraging and motivating. I also sought out opportunities within the organization. For example, I was one of six employees accepted into their North Carolina Leadership Development Program. I enrolled in an MBA program and I also attempted to start an honors fraternity on campus. The initial excitement I had for my job eventually wore off, though, and I eagerly awaited other opportunities.

Two and a half years from the day I started at UOPx, I was promoted to Operations Supervisor. The Opts position placed me in more of a leadership role, and I worked with some awesome employees. I was accepted into another leadership program, completed my MBA, and started teaching undergraduate business courses in the evenings. Despite my extracurricular activities at work, I grew restless again and yearned to pursue a position more in line with my passions of teaching, training, and speaking. I was promoted again three years later to Regional Trainer.

The trainer position was particularly attractive to me because it allowed me to do what I loved, speaking to large and small crowds of people and changing lives. The selection process was six months long. When I finally received an offer for the position, I found out that the trainer position I applied for in Charlotte, NC about 200 miles away was filled. Instead, I was offered the same trainer position almost 600 miles away in Nashville, TN.

I took the job and was fortunate to work alongside a group of dynamic individuals spread throughout the southeastern part of the country. That same year I started my new job in a new state, I got married, and I had my first child. I was also in the process of completing my Ph.D. program, which had been a four and a half year endeavor so far. My wife quit her job to be at home full time with our newborn son, and I concentrated a great deal of effort on my new position, which I enjoyed. It was an eventful year, to say the least. Because of all I had accomplished, I felt successful.

I was working on some high-profile projects and garnering some positive attention from work. Between work and school, though, I had little time for my new family. I told myself it was worth it and reminded myself that this is the dedication needed to get ahead in life.

My wife graciously supported me in my career and educational pursuits, even though they monopolized my time. One day, I received an email from HR informing me they wanted to talk to me personally about a new organization-wide initiative. I had already worked on some interesting and rewarding initiatives in my new role, so I was excited about what laid ahead.

A couple of days later, the HR representative called me first thing that morning for our scheduled phone appointment. The HR representative proceeded to tell me that the new initiative was nothing I would be working on. In fact, the new initiative left me with no job. It turned out that UOPx was downsizing, and I was being laid off. The minute I hung up the phone, a director came to my office door to escort me out of the building as though it was all a mundane routine. I had seen other employees be fired or laid off before, but having it happen to me was surreal. I had always had a job, so the thought of not having a job to go to the next day was terrifying.

Initially, I went into panic mode and quickly scrambled to find a new job. I used just about every job search engine you can imagine. I contacted old colleagues on LinkedIn, as well as recruiters. Most of the jobs I was interested in required a terminal degree, which I had not yet completed. Months went by with little progress and very few interviews.

It seemed like there were no viable opportunities available to me. That's when the doubt sets in: "Maybe I should settle for something less. Maybe I don't deserve the job of my dreams. Maybe pursuing my degree has been a waste of time." Have you ever had any thoughts like these before? These thoughts promote fear and uncertainty, which can cause you to be idle. I was holding my breath hoping an opportunity would come my way.

I started to feel like I was no longer a success. My dilemma made me question how success could be so fleeting. If I was a success one day when I had a job, was I now unsuccessful after being laid off? Would you consider yourself successful if you were unemployed? Because I didn't notice any opportunities around me, I didn't make any progress toward any of my goals. I had essentially let my situation debilitate me. I needed to reflect and rediscover my definition of success in life before I could move forward.

The elements of Breathing Success are:

- Recognize that opportunity is everywhere, like the air we breathe

- Inhale opportunities

- Exhale results

- Avoid foul air

- Keep at it and breathe easy

Chapter 2

Owning Your Breath

"When you own your breath, no one can steal your peace." ~
Unknown

I once heard the argument that if you are successful at one thing you will be a failure at something else. For example, if you're a successful CEO of a fortune 500 company the time and energy you put into that role will take away from your ability to be a good parent. What do you think?

How do you know when you are successful in life? Take a moment to reflect on how you formulated your definition of success. Are you successful in life once you have obtained a certain amount of money? How about when you have a particular position at work? Do fame, fortune, or accolades define your idea of success in life? In this day and age, especially in the U.S, people have a rapacious appetite for stuff.

This behavior has been accelerated by corporate America, promoted by the media, and generally accepted by society at large. But is the acquiring of stuff synonymous with success? Knowing how to define success is important if you are going to obtain it. I found success early on, when I hardly had a dollar to my name.

Taking My First Breath

My introduction to higher education began at Wake Technical Community College. After a less than stellar year at Wake Tech, I took some time off to decide whether college was for me. During my time off, I lived with my parents and worked at a record store. I had lots of free time and few responsibilities. I was having a lot of fun during my time away from school and working full-time. Coincidentally, I encountered the most interesting people while working at this archaic store. I met lawyers, entrepreneurs, doctors, DJs, musicians, and college students.

Although they were all pursuing very different endeavors, I noticed a couple of things they all had in common. They were all doing something they enjoyed and actively striving toward their goals. I met a lawyer who had his own practice and was able to spend time fixing up motorcycles on the side. He would ride his BMW motorcycle to the store every now and then. I met a DJ who was passionate about music. He started his own record label and signed a couple of artists.

I also met two young ladies who both wanted to pursue careers in law some day and they had just enrolled in UNC Greensboro. At the time I had aspirations of finishing college and becoming an attorney. These encounters made me realize that I was not doing anything I truly enjoyed and I was not striving toward any of my goals. This is when I began to breathe success without even knowing it.

Although I was having fun, I had an emptiness inside that was not being fulfilled by my frivolous pursuits. In the back of my head, I knew that if I kept doing more of what I was currently doing, I would not get any closer to my goals. I had a feeling that I was not where I was supposed to be, and I knew I could be doing more. Ultimately, I was not at peace. Does this sound familiar?

Fast forward three years; I was a senior at UNC Greensboro and working as the Student Attorney General. This was an appointed position with UNC Greensboro's student government in which I supervised staff who adjudicated student hearings. I was also making less money than I did at the ancient store....I mean the record store. I lived in a tiny dorm room. My academic and volunteer obligations left me with very little free time, and I had a ton of responsibilities. I still had unfulfilled goals. I had not earned my degree or obtained a full-time job, and I was nowhere close to making the money I wanted to earn. Despite all of that, I was fulfilled and at peace.

My experience of meeting those people while working at the record store helped me to recognize the opportunities around me. I was able to focus on what I wanted, recognize the opportunities available to me, and take action. More importantly, I was consistent with my progress, and every day I got closer to finishing school and becoming an attorney. I knew that if I kept doing more of what I was doing, I would eventually reach my goal of finishing school and becoming an attorney.

I knew that for the meantime, I was where I was supposed to be, doing what I was supposed to be doing. I felt successful simply because I was pursing my goals. Most importantly, the peace that I had was an indication that I was successful. This experience showed me that I could create my own definition of success. This experience shaped my idea of success and it was almost as if I just took my first breath.

The Definition of Breathing Success

Before we proceed any further, let us take a moment to establish a working definition of success. How would you define success? If you are like most people, society has imprinted upon you the notion that wealth, status, accolades, and material items define our success. While you can be successful in obtaining these things, I would argue that you can be just as successful without obtaining any of those things.

Our body is capable of doing many things. Some of the more ancillary abilities such as wiggling your fingers or walking are great, but not necessary to live. Taking in oxygen is necessary to live. Attaining money and nice things is like wiggling your fingers and walking. Breathing success is a necessary practice that can bring you peace. According to the Oxford Dictionary, success is defined as:

1) The accomplishment of an aim; a favorable outcome.

2) The attainment of wealth, fame, or position.

3) A thing or person that turns out well.

The second definition is the furthest from the definition we will be working with. While you can certainly be successful in obtaining the items in the second definition, those items do not define your success. We will not be working from the premise that you are only successful if you attain wealth, fame, or a particular position. The first and third definitions are closer to the one we want, but it is not quite what we are looking for. The definition we will be working with is as follows:

Success is being at peace with where you are in life.

I know what you're thinking: this definition seems too philosophical, spiritual, or abstract. It also does not sound as sexy as Oxford Dictionary's second definition. The attainment of wealth, fame, and position, is initially more appealing than the attainment of peace. Peace can go out the window if I can have a six-figure salary, a five-bedroom house, and four luxury cars in the driveway, right? Well, if peace equals success and not the other materialistic things, then why do we spend our time and energy chasing after these things?

I think we can agree that most people believe once we attain these items we will be successful and happy. But I'm sure you have heard the old adage that money doesn't buy you happiness. This really is true to a certain extent. Studies show that money can increase one's happiness when it elevates an individual out of poverty, but once your salary reaches a certain point (usually the national average) and your basic needs are met (i.e. food, clothing, stable residence, etc.), then more money causes little to no increase in happiness.

Just about anyone reading this who is not already monetarily wealthy might be thinking that this notion is preposterous. Surely if you significantly increase your wealth, you will be happier. The truth is that you might be for a while, but then you will begin to adjust to your new lifestyle. Once you have adjusted to your new lifestyle, you will have a desire for even more money and possessions than you do now, and the feeling of emptiness will return. This never-ending cycle is called "hedonic adaptation," or the "hedonic treadmill."

For example, your body only needs to inhale and exhale about 7 to 8 liters a minute to properly function; anything beyond that is superfluous. There's always more air to breathe, but yet you only take what you need with one breath at a time. Aiming for a goal that can only bring short-term satisfaction does not seem so appealing any more, does it? Regardless of your current socioeconomic status, the attainment of wealth and expensive items will not bring you long-term happiness, and you will ultimately feel unsuccessful in life despite your success in attaining those specific material goals.

Aiming for more money leads to a lose/lose situation. Your options are to have the money and material things, causing you to eventually feel empty from wanting more, or else never have the money and material things and feel empty without them. Either option means not being at peace with where you are in life. Most people would probably think, "I would rather take my chances with the money and take it from there." But before you go and sign up for The Price Is Right, let's give peace a chance.

Give Peace a Chance

When I was a manager, my employees had to monitor their time to ensure they did not work over 40 hours each week. In the beginning, I would work with them to resolve any time discrepancies and coordinate coverage when necessary. I used to tell my employees that, when bringing a problem to my attention, they should always be prepared to offer a solution. Eventually, they resolved time discrepancies and coordinated coverage on their own and simply kept me in the communication loop.

I say that to reassure you that I do not intend to criticize the aforementioned way of thinking without offering an alternative. Earlier we established that attainment of peace in one's life is the definition of success. Instead of looking for wealth, fame, or position, to define your success, I would suggest *peace*.

Yes, peace; as in the state of harmony with every element of your own life and your surroundings. Wealth, fame, or positions aren't worth the air you breathe. Here are a few reasons why you might want to consider making peace your aim in life.

One reason you would want to incorporate peace into your sense of what it means to be successful is that wealth, fame, or position are all potential goals under the larger umbrella of peace. When you are at peace, you are already on the right path in life, and you will complete some of the goals you deem important in life along the way.

If you go about attaining success the other way, arbitrarily choosing goals that you think will make you successful, you run the risk of continuing the feeling of emptiness inside despite the fact you were successful in obtaining wealth, fame, or position. This may include wealth, position, honors, or another desires of yours. There is nothing wrong with wanting wealth, position, and honors, but these are potential byproducts of attaining peace.

The process of attaining peace reaches far beyond wealth and lavish items. Being at peace could also include relationships in your life, hobbies, or your diet; it encompasses every aspect of how you live your life. Take a moment to think about the areas in your life where you would like to improve; focus on areas that are not tied to acquiring money or items.

More than likely, you have goals, and reaching for peace covers the entire gamut of those goals. When you reach goals or are in the process of reaching goals, you have a positive feeling because you know you are on the right path. Simply put, when you do *good*, you feel *good!*

As we discussed before, wealth, fame, and position are moving targets. There will always be more money to earn, more fame to gain, and more positions to attain. Once you reach a certain level or status, that new level eventually becomes your new normal. The hedonic treadmill turns, and you keep pressing on, unsatisfied. By contrast, when you are at peace with your life, you are content in the moment.

You would still be a success even if you temporarily or permanently lose the money and lavish things, because those things were merely the byproducts of your pursuit of peace, not your actual goal. Success is attained in the constant pursuit of your goal. Your life is filled with meaningful pursuits and the process of reaching the goals is just as fulfilling as the attainment of the goal.

Keep in mind that meaningful pursuits are going to vary depending on the individual. Some people may not have any career aspirations or desire to earn advanced degrees. Others are not spiritual, or don't care to improve their social lives. At the same time, your feelings about the aforementioned pursuits may change as you mature.

Your sense of success evolves as you do. Your goals at ages 15, 25, and 55 are very different. Yet you are not left with the empty or dissatisfied feeling as your goals become commensurate with your maturation.

You won't always reach your goals, but you can always *try* to reach them. Striving for and maintaining the state of peace requires you to be in constant motion. If you are truly striving for what it is you want, you are always where you are supposed to be in life. Martin Luther King Jr. was a good example of this. His success did not derive from a goal he obtained, rather his persistence in striving for the meaningful endeavors that he dedicated his life to. In essence, you enjoy your unique and evolving *journey* independent of society's restricting definition of success.

Lastly, attaining peace is an all-encompassing goal that can apply to every facet of your life. Having peace does not mean that everything will be perfect. Even though you are at peace, you will still experience challenges, obstacles, and frustrations in life. The benefit of attaining peace is the opportunity to handle life's challenges more efficiently because of your new state of being.

Have you ever had difficulty breathing from strenuous activity? The moment you had a second to rest, what was the first thing you did? Catch your breath, right? The physical activity may be challenging, but you knew if you could catch your breath, you'd have a chance to continue. The process I will share for attaining peace in life will help you solve problems more effectively and make you more confident to take on new ventures. You think more money or items will help you with life's challenges in the same way? I've seen people obtain more money, but not peace.

I once knew a gentleman who acquired a significant amount of money in a short amount of time. We will call him Tony. Tony, worked in sales and doubled his salary in less than three years. Tony did not necessarily care for his job and sometimes made unethical decisions at work, but he liked the money and the lavish items it afforded him.

He purchased a brand new white 2010 Mercedes-Benz C300 Sport and a black 2009 Ford Explorer Eddie Bauer in the same year. He also kept his previous vehicle, a 2007 Honda Accord. He purchased a single family home the next year. Tony wore very expensive clothes such as Armani and Guess to work.

He made it clear what he wanted to purchase and went out and got it. Sound good so far? Tony was also single and a ladies' man. He was already paying child support for his only child from a previous relationship, which admittedly wasn't much of a financial hardship for him due to his hefty salary.

Tony began dating a coworker, and then a few months later, while still involved with her, took a liking to another coworker. We can refer to them as Coworker A and Coworker B. I assume he had to do the same to keep things straight in his head. Anyway, when Coworker A found out about Coworker B's involvement with Tony, drama ensued at work. The drama and some of the unethical decisions he made led to several write-ups, and eventually Tony's termination. The resulting lack of income made it difficult for Tony to pay for his automobiles, new house, and the other trappings of his lavish lifestyle. The plot thickened when Tony found out that Coworker A would be having his child. Now Tony's house is in foreclosure; he has sold both of his newer vehicles, and he is paying child support for two children.

If Tony's success is tied to having money or things, then he is no longer successful. This is a recipe for disaster. Tony's goals in life were centered on items that were ultimately trivial. If he had prioritized his goals to be consistent with reaching peace, he might be better off today. For example, one of his goals in life could have been to be the best at his current position, which could have prevented him from being terminated from work. If his other goal was focused on building meaningful relationships with those who matter the most to him, he might have just chosen one woman at a time. Maybe he was thinking the more, the merrier.

The Notorious B.I.G was definitely on to something when he said "Mo money, mo problems." Until I hear the song Mo peace, mo problems, I will posit that peace is the way to go. Have you ever achieved a goal that ultimately turned out to be a waste of your time? Think long and hard about how you spend your energy. To breathe success, you'll want to take intentional breaths. You don't want to inhale anything just to find out you inhaled carbon monoxide.

Think about a goal you have successfully reached that was worth attaining. Maybe you earned a degree, took a trip out of the country, or started a business. I'll assume you were excited once you achieved your goal. But think about how you felt while in the process of pursuing the goal. How did you feel when you could see that you were making progress toward your goal? Let's say your goal was to save $5000 in six months to take a trip out of the country. It probably felt good to look at your account after three months and see that you had saved up $2500. Even though you hadn't gone on the trip or even saved the full $5000 yet, the progress you made felt good. You knew that, if you kept saving, you would eventually reach your goal.

Think about the flipside of this concept. How would you feel if three months had gone by and you had little or no money saved? You would feel defeated. Even though the six months were not up yet, you would know that you were going down a path that would not produce the results you desired.

This feeling might even cause you to give up. Have you ever given up on reaching a goal before? Think about the conditions or reasons that led you to give up on reaching your goal. Proper planning can greatly increase your chances of reaching your goals.

Your Breathing Pattern

I got into jogging a few years ago after one of my previous employers participated in a 5k walk for breast cancer. The first time I participated was in October of 2009 and I was dead tired from walking 3.1 miles up and down small hills. Yes, I said walking 3.1 miles almost killed me and I was just 28 years old at the time.

After my questionable performance, I set a goal to jog the entire 3.1 miles nonstop at the same event the next year. With all of the training I did on my own to prepare for the event, focusing on my breathing helped the most.

I obtained a gym membership at a facility near my home.

Three days a week I jogged on a treadmill and did intervals of walking and running for an hour; it was challenging. My feet would start to hurt, then my legs, and eventually I started to feel a sharp pain on my right side which felt like someone just stabbed me with a fork. Not to mention I was sweating profusely.

I used to hate it when the sweat from my forehead would run down into my eye, causing a burning sensation. Imagine me on the treadmill constantly blinking from desperately trying to get the sweat of my eye, while onlookers think I am winking at them.

In any case, I noticed the pain I felt in my side while I was jogging greatly subsided when I focused on my breathing. When I focused on taking consistent, long breaths, I was able to run for a longer period of time. I also noticed, once I took my focus off of my breathing I started to slowly feel the pain in my muscles from running.

I trained for about 7 months for the 5K and in October of 2010 I reached my goal. I completed the 3.1 miles while jogging nonstop. I completed the event in just over 30 minutes. I know my completion time is not very impressive, but it was a significant improvement from the year before. Think about it, focusing on something as basic as breathing helped me to overcome a major physical challenge.

My breathing pattern set the tone for how I reached my goal of jogging 3.1 miles. Your breathing pattern in life is essentially your detailed plan for how you're going to reach your goals. It sets the pace for your actions in the quest for success. Breathing patterns consist of a goal, milestones, and corresponding resources which is illustrated on the next page.

```
┌─────────────────────────┐
│        Success          │
└─────────────────────────┘
```

```
     ▲              ▲              ▲
    ╱ ╲            ╱ ╲            ╱ ╲
   Breathing     Breathing      Breathing
   Pattern 1     Pattern 2      Pattern 3

     Goal           Goal           Goal

   Milestones     Milestones     Milestones

   Resources      Resources      Resources
```

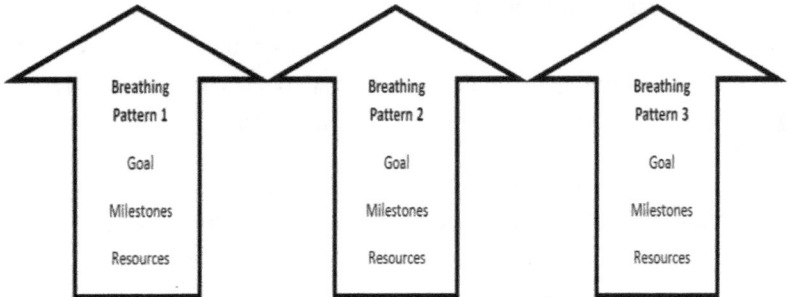

Your breathing pattern begins with creating your goal statements. You'll first want to make sure you don't overextend yourself or your resources. The law of diminishing returns applies to your breathing pattern. This law states that, in a productive process, adding more than one factor of production, while holding all others constant, will at some point yield lower returns.

For example, imagine a farmer who manually works his land to produce a crop for sale. If the farmer purchases fertilizer for his crop, it can improve crop production. If the farmer continues to increase the amount of fertilizer used on the farm, at some point the fertilizer's effect on the yield will begin to decease. Also, the increasing cost will begin to outweigh the potential profit made from the yield.

The same can be said for strategizing to complete your life's goals. In other words, you'll want to focus your time and attention on a smaller number of goals so that you might potentially yield a greater success rate, rather than focusing on so many goals that nothing gets done. Take one breath at a time because you're running the marathon known as life.

It has been noted by economists that if you focus on three objectives, you'll be likely to succeed in all three. If you attempt four to ten objectives, you'll succeed in one or two. And if you attempt more than ten objectives, you'll succeed in none. This formula suggests that a person should not focus on any more than three goals at a time. Once you've achieved one of your three goals, you can replace it with another. This will allow you to maintain your maximum efficiency level on a consistent basis. You'll also naturally change your goals as you mature.

Take a moment and think about a goal that you are in the process of pursuing. How do you know whether you're making progress toward that goal? I stated earlier that, in order to maximize your chances of achieving your goals, you should be pursing no more than three goals at a time.

Now you need to formulate and decide upon your three goals. We come up with goals all the time. It's common for us to come with goals that are actually impossible for us to attain.

For example, we set the too-vague goal of getting a new job. Or we set a goal without limits, such as the goal of having a bigger place for one's family to live in. Instead, we ought to set goals with the SMART acronym in mind: Specific, Measureable, Attainable, Relevant, and Timely. There are a several variations on this acronym, but in this book we will use the variation on the next page.

SMART Goals

- **S**pecific: Target precisely what you want.

- **Me**asureable: Determine the indicator of progress.

- **A**ttainable: Be sure that this goal can be achieved, given the available resources.

- **R**elevant: Decide that the goal is worth the effort of pursuing.

- **T**imely: Determine the timeframe in which the goal should be achieved.

When you create a goal, it should meet these criteria. I imagine some people might not be up to the challenge of being this thorough in writing a goal, but taking the time to make sure your goal meets these criteria can save you a lot of time and effort in the end. Why would you want to make breathing any more difficult than it has to be? After all, if the goal is that important to you, it is worthwhile to make sure you take the proper steps to reach it. Smart goals help you become more intentional with each breath.

Using a previous or current goal, practice writing a goal statement on page 89. Once you feel comfortable with your goal statement, write three finalized goals on pages 90 - 92. The three goals you write down will become the beginnings of your breathing patterns. For example, one of your goals could be to start your own business or become more social. If so, be specific. What kind of business? When would you like to officially open your doors? What does social mean to you, or how will you measure it? A correctly written goal statement answers such questions. Eventually you'll get to the point where you only need to write out goal statements for your more complex goals.

Example Goal Statement: My online retail clothing business will be fully operational and registered by December 1, 2015.

We will complete the rest of the breathing pattern in Chapter Four. Take a moment to imagine what your life would look like if you were actively pursuing everything you wanted in life. Even though you may not have everything right now, you are already well on your way if you are formulating SMART goals. You can have faith that if you keep doing more of what you are doing, you will have a realistic chance at reaching all of your goals.

Most importantly, it is energizing to work on something you're passionate about. This type of productivity toward a life you want will bring you peace. You ultimately want to live a life filled with more meaningful pursuits than meaningless pursuits. When you live your life successfully, you are successful in life. This process should be as easy and comfortable to you as breathing.

Success: is being at peace with where you are in life.

Chapter 3

Inhaling Opportunities

"When you want wisdom and insight as badly as you want to breathe, it is then you shall have it." ~ *Socrates*

In order to break down the basics of being successful in life, this book focuses on the process of breathing. You would think the process of inhaling and exhaling would be effortless. You are doing it right now as you read these very words, for goodness sake. And as easy as this process may seem, sometimes we still forget to breathe. Think about common instances when people have to remind each other to breathe. People remind us to breathe when we become angry, afraid, physically or mentally stressed, or nervous. Breathing is especially important while participating in activities such as deep sea diving, sky diving, jogging or running, yoga, and giving birth.

Breathing seems simple enough, and yet we forget to do it when we need to the most. The same holds true for being successful. Every day we forget to do the simple things that can potentially make us successful. The process of breathing success is similar to breathing oxygen. We need to focus on our breathing to be successful in life. This chapter will discuss how to identify opportunities for success.

Opportunity is in the Air

I had been working at University of Phoenix for a little over three months when I first heard about the North Carolina Leadership Development Program (NCLDP). Employees who worked there for at least three months were eligible to apply for this leadership program. The selection committee chose participants who would collaborate on a high-level project. Being accepted to the program would give the employees exposure to upper management and other parts of the organization. Acceptance would also look good on a résumé and could get them noticed by current and future employers. I was still fairly new to the organization, but I applied anyway.

One day, my manager asked me to accompany him to a local transcript evaluation conference. I went, and thought nothing of it until a week later my manager wanted me to present the conference material in his stead at the next staff meeting. Nervous, I frantically put together the best PowerPoint presentation I could. I presented the material at the staff meeting without passing out, and the only thought that ran through my head afterwards was, "I'm glad that's over." About a week later I was excited to learn that I had been accepted into the NCLDP.

I was the least tenured and youngest employee accepted into the program that year. I could not explain why I was chosen. A few weeks later, one of the members of the selection committee told me that I was the last member selected to the program. She also told me that the decision was made when one of the senior directors saw my transcript evaluation presentation at the staff meeting.

A mundane duty inadvertently turned into an opportunity— and that was not the last time this happened. I have been offered opportunities after a presentation or speech on many occasions. The opportunities have come to me as though I am an opportunity magnet. Think about the opportunities that I might have been able to capitalize on if I would have actively reached out to the audience members after every presentation or speech. This is a common practice for me today. The fact is that opportunity is everywhere; we just have to get better at recognizing it.

Before we dive into identifying opportunities, you have to understand how opportunities work. Opportunities are limited to your creativity and persistence at seeking them out. Once you change your perspective, you will notice opportunities all around you.

Opportunities are almost everywhere, like fresh air. When you're in an environment not conducive to breathing, you automatically gravitate toward fresh air, don't you? Think about when you drive by a landfill or walk past a group of smokers. Your body yearns for fresh air.

An opportunity is a condition or situation favorable to attaining a goal. Creativity and persistence can create the conditions necessary to produce opportunities. Once an opportunity is present, it is up to the individual to recognize the opportunity and "breathe" it in. When you actively seek an opportunity, there will be a reaction. This concept is consistent with Sir Isaac Newton's third law of physics: "To every action there is always an equal and opposite reaction."

Notice that, before you can expect an equal and opposite reaction, you must first initiate the action. The action is what you can control. When you put yourself out there, let people know who you are, and make it known what your intentions are, things can happen. In other words, if you take action, you can expect a reaction.

Opportunity is everywhere…literally, everywhere! The skeptics are looking around right now thinking "Oh really, Dauv?

Where?" The optimists are thinking "Oh really, Dauv? I wonder where my opportunity is hiding?" Most people, places, and things can potentially be an opportunity for you to achieve your goal and be successful in life. You will need to learn to train your mind to identify opportunities until seeing them becomes second nature.

Although breathing is second nature to us, the process is actually quite complex. When the body takes in air or inhales, the diaphragm contracts or flattens. The volume of your body, especially of your lungs, expands. Your thorax, abdomen, and diaphragm are all involved in the process of inhaling oxygen. It is amazing that this can be done involuntarily or even unconsciously.

We consciously practice breathing when participating in some of the activities mentioned earlier, such as deep sea diving or yoga. There must be a good reason why people practice this basic bodily function. Breathing is one of the most basic and visceral acts for the human body. To deny your body air is to deny yourself the opportunity to do anything else.

You'll need to practice identifying opportunities on a regular basis. I am going to channel my inner Allen Iverson and emphasize the word *practice*: "We're talking about practice." Yes, people. The same way people practice the art of taking in air, you will need to do the same with identifying opportunity to give yourself a better chance of being successful. Let us examine some core concepts that can help you identify potential opportunities.

Your body and lungs' process of expanding to take in air is similar to the actions you take to increase your capacity to notice opportunities. The practices below will allow you to expand your capacity for opportunities presented to you.

Inhale Opportunities

Step 1: Train your brain to notice what you want

Step 2: Make time for your passion

Step 3: Connect with people

Visualize

I don't care who you are, it would be extremely difficult for anyone to recognize opportunity without knowing what he or she wants in life. It's no wonder that one must first visualize a goal before being able to recognize the opportunities in life. There is a part of your brain called the Reticular Activating System, or RAS, that can assist you in recognizing opportunities. The RAS senses things around you and categorizes them based on its positive or negative impact on you.

For example, if you were attacked by a dog when you were a child, your brain will remember that experience and the animal responsible. You might unconsciously be on the lookout for dogs behaving in the same manner so you could avoid them. Conversely, if you were really excited when you purchased your first car, which was a white, '96 Corolla, you'll notice that car from then on.

Now that I've mentioned a white, '96 Corolla, don't be surprised if in the course of the next week or two, you notice a white, '96 Corolla while you're driving, watching TV, surfing the internet, or even when someone mentions it. (I promise not to buy white, '96 Corolla just to prove a point.) Along the same lines, have you ever noticed when you purchase a new car you seem to notice that same car on the road a lot more than you did before? That's also the RAS at work.

The RAS is unconsciously at work sorting information out and in this case finding similarities with vehicles. Your brain is automatically looking for items of interest in the world. I always picture a police-tracking dog smelling the object before zeroing in on its objective. Everyone's RAS will identify perceived opportunities based on your experiences. It's much easier to breathe the fresh air of opportunities once you've identified what those are for you.

Vision Board

Training your brain to search for what you want in life is not as difficult as it may seem. There are many methods to do this, but one effective way is to create a vision board. A vision board is a collage usually composed of illustrations and images that symbolize what the creator deems important. If this sounds strange to you, not to worry; I was initially skeptical too. I gave it a try on a small scale before being completely sold on the idea. I was stuck in a dead-end sales job right out of college before this process helped me find new job opportunities.

One day, I was flipping through a magazine when I saw a picture of a young professional. He was a young man wearing a stylish suit and holding a briefcase in his hand. The photographer had caught him mid-stride, making it look as though he was on the go. This picture encapsulated where I wanted to be in the near future. I cut that picture out and placed in the top drawer of my temporary desk at work. I would take it out of my desk drawer each day and bring it with me to whichever new station I was assigned to work. Every time I opened the drawer to get a stapler or pen, I would see that picture. It reminded me to continue looking for the next career opportunity. This reminder came in especially handy on the days when I was feeling complacent with my surroundings. A few months after cutting out that picture, I did find the opportunity I was passionate about.

The visual was effective in helping me find the opportunity I was looking for because it kept me focused on an image that represented what I was pursuing. It made me much more aware and efficient when looking for potential career opportunities. The experience sold me on the concept of vision boards, and I created one soon after I found my new job. I have since become much more adept at noticing opportunities that can get me closer to the life I want.

My wife and I enjoyed creating our vision board. We divided it into three sections: family, lifestyle, and career. The family section has pictures that represent what my wife and I want for our family. For example, we included a picture of my wife and me on our wedding day to remind us of that day and why we got married. We also cut out the word "healthy children" because we want to emphasize healthy living to our children.

The lifestyle section includes pictures of places we would like to travel to and where we'd like to live. We have a picture of the Great Pyramids of Giza because my wife and I have always wanted to travel to Egypt. The career section is composed of pictures and words that describe our criteria for our careers. We included a picture of a well-decorated and organized home office because we both enjoy working from home.

We also cut out a phrase in a magazine that read, "Good things come to those that work hard." Looking at our vision board every day reminds my wife and me of some of the things we have and are still working for.

A vision board is not difficult to make and can even be fun once you get into it. I'm not the arts and crafts kind of guy, but I enjoyed locating visual representations of what I wanted my life to look like. All you need is a piece of poster board, some pictures from magazines or printed from online, and an adhesive such as glue, tape, or staples to stick the pictures to the board. There are probably a lot of things you want out of life, but you'll need a starting point.

The first three goals that you formulated starting on page 90 would make a great starting point. For example, if one of your goals is to start a business, find a picture of what that job looks like in your imagination. What would your office or work environment look like? What types of tasks would you do on a regular basis? What would you be required to wear? You would essentially answer these questions and more with the visual representations on your vision board.

The visuals are fairly easy to obtain. People typically use magazines, but if you have access to a printer there are unlimited pictures on the internet. You'll want to use images that represent the lifestyle you want. I know someone who used a picture of a monkey wearing khaki pants. The picture reminders her to be creative at work. You can be as simple or eclectic as you'd like.

As you reach your goals and create new ones you can add images to your vision board. Try to focus on the big picture. Once you've completed your vision board, put in a highly visible place. My wife and I keep our shared vision board right outside our bedroom so that we see it every morning when we step out of our room. This is relatively painless method for training your brain to notice opportunities. You'll be more prone to gravitate to fresh air once you know where it is.

Your Passion is Your Purpose

I can almost anticipate the eye rolling that will ensue after you read this subheading. That's ok, I rolled my eyes too as I was typing it. Admittedly, it does sound a bit cheesy, but it works. Your passion almost acts as a compass to success. Most people have something they are passionate about.

Spending time doing what you enjoy can bring you satisfaction, and if you train your mind correctly, the RAS is looking for ways to do it more. It's a step in the right direction to finding opportunities more easily.

Following your passion sounds so irresponsible, doesn't it? But who says so? Think about one of your hobbies you currently enjoy. When you're doing something you enjoy, you tend to be happier. You're more relaxed, and your personality shines. You tend to work harder and put forth more effort.

When you're in this state of mind, you are more susceptible to noticing opportunities. I'm not saying your passion has to be your profession, but you should indulge in your passion on a regular basis. And if you're able to turn that passion into a career, that's a bonus!

I had a co-worker who was able to experience this firsthand. Let's call her Sara. Sara made good money at her recruiting job, but she got absolutely no joy from it. She did, however, love dogs. She had a dog of her own and would always volunteer to dog-sit when she had the chance. She eventually began volunteering at the local dog shelter. She even took in stray dogs and nursed them back to health. I used to poke fun at her and call her the "dog whisperer." Regardless of whether others found her passion odd, she spent increasingly more time around dogs.

As Sara spent more time doing what she enjoyed, she became noticeably happier in life. The time she spent doing something she enjoyed began to outweigh the 40 hours a week she spent at work. She would sometimes complain that the careers that would allow her to work with dogs would not pay anywhere near what she made in her marketing job.

After a couple of years, though, Sara was laid off. After pondering her next step for a few months, she saw an opportunity to open her own K9 boarding house. She was fortunate enough to make time doing something she enjoyed. Converting that passion into a career was a bonus.

Whatever your passion is, there is more than likely some type of organization, activity, or group that can allow you to further explore your passion. If someone is having a convention for something you're passionate about, you need to be there. If there's a local group that meets to discuss something you're passionate about, you need to be there. These days, it's easy to find groups on meetup.com that meet for all kinds of reasons.

I am passionate about public speaking and leadership. One evening while listing to NPR news, the reporter mentioned Toastmasters. I researched Toastmasters online and learned it was an organization dedicated to working on public speaking and leadership. I attended my first meeting a couple of weeks later and joined a local club the following week. I've been a member now for over five years. I have participated in and won many speech contests, connected with great people, and learned a lot.

When you pursue your passion, you'll grow, and the experience will entice you to do even more things you're passionate about. You'll eventually get to the point where you'll spend a significant amount of time engaging in activities you enjoy. I know this may sound far-fetched, but I challenge you to give it a try first. You might know someone who works, volunteers, or engages in activities they're passionate about. I know quite a few, and they are quite content with their lives; especially the individuals who earn a living pursuing their passion. Pursuing your passion can help you meet like-minded people. This can be energizing and encourage you to do more with your passion. This was the case with Sara. Sara's friends at the dog shelter helped her realize her goal of opening the K9 boarding house. She was able to identify her fresh air and gravitate to it more when it presented itself. Her passion gave her purpose. Meeting people, like-minded or not, can always be beneficial. Next, I'll highlight the importance of connecting with others.

Connect with a Purpose

Connecting with other people is a powerful technique that involves more than just networking. When you connect, you can open yourself up to more opportunities. Many opportunities indirectly or directly begin with a people. One of my mentors is a prime example of this. Have you ever hung out with a "Mr. or Ms. Popular" who seems to know everyone? Barry, one of my ex-coworkers, is the epitome of that person. Barry is retired military and has been in sales and recruitment for over 25 years. He was a regional director of business development for a large corporation and is now an entrepreneur. He is and has always been in the business of connecting with people.

Years ago, Barry and I took a trip to Virginia to attend our first doctoral residency. Doctoral students, faculty, and school staff were attending from all around the country. We both arrived essentially not knowing anyone but each other. On the first day of residency Barry and I went to the dining hall to eat. Barry got out of line with his food first so I told him I'd catch up and find him once I got my food. I stepped out of the line looking for Barry sitting by himself and instead found him in the middle of a half dozen students he just met laughing and carrying on. The next evening Barry was a hit at the student mixer socializing and dancing in the center of a crowd of cheering onlookers.

Barry and I were in separate programs so we mostly attended separate sessions, but every time I ran into him in the hall he would be talking to someone new. On the drive back from Virginia Barry had well over 50 business cards from all the new students, faculty, and staff he connected with. He told me stories about how he met them, what they did, and more importantly the new opportunities he had access to. I think I might have met five other students and two faculty members. And while I had a good time, I did not leave with as many new opportunities as Barry did.

People are one of the best resources to utilize in the quest for success, but you must first connect with them. You are also a potential resource because of your background, expertise, education, and skills.

Think about standing in the middle of one of the busiest places in America. For me, Wall Street comes to mind. Think about how many people are walking around Wall Street on an average weekday. These people are brokering deals, crunching numbers, making purchases, and connecting with other people. Think about how much closer you could be to your goal if half of those people were willing to help you achieve your goals. They could be if you were to connect with them. Odds are they're doing at least one thing for someone else on any given day even if it does benefit themselves; why can't that one thing be for you?

Networking is the interacting between people who share common interests and who exchange ideas and resources. Is it just me, or can networking be a little awkward sometimes? Like being on a blind date, networking puts you in situations that can be uncomfortable as you talk with complete strangers. Breathing success can be difficult when you're holding your breath assuming the other person has bad breath. This means you might refrain from inhaling opportunities because you are unsure what the other person has to offer or vice versa.

You may find yourself searching for questions to ask after the first couple of minutes of conversation. Maybe there are a few awkward moments of silence. Networking also tends to have a professional connotation to it, which can be intimidating to some. This can be an intimidating prospect, especially for introverts.

Introverts are a peculiar bunch. I'm an introvert myself until I have an audience to speak to. Introverts should remember that other people may have something you need in order to achieve your goal. If your goal is clear, then the actions you need to take are clear. Yet connecting is necessary and highly productive as you seek to reach your goals. Two heads are better than one when looking for fresh air. If networking has never been your thing, you should try finding your own way to connect with others.

Connecting:

- Identify commonality between you and the other person.

- Determine the other person's strength(s) and goal(s).

- Identify ways you can help them achieve their goal(s).

- Identify ways they can help you achieve your goal(s).

- Stay in touch with them periodically.

Connecting with a purpose requires maintaining relationships with individuals after you've identified their strengths and goals. You can connect with others in just about any environment. You can be at work, a networking event, church, any social gathering, or really anywhere. This method structures your conversation and gives your intentions to connect sincere meaning.

When connecting with others, you'll want to go a step further than the generic conversations you may be used to having. To do this, you'll first want to find some commonality. Maybe you are from the same city, went to the same high school, or like the same sport. What are some of your personal interests? Whatever your interests are, talking about your personal interests can help you naturally become more personable when meeting someone for the first time. People are more likely to be forthcoming about themselves with others they can identify with. The goal is to find out what the other person's strengths and goals are.

Next, you'll want to find out what the person does well. A person's strengths might be tied to his or her profession, education, hobby, personality, or another aspect of who the person is. Ultimately, what gives this person strength, or how is this person gifted? I've found success by asking what people's goals are or what they hope to accomplish personally or professionally. You may find a person's goals or strengths are tied to their personal interests. I'll follow up with asking them what do they do well that will help them reach their goal.

When you find out what their goals are, you'll know how you can help them. Conversely, when you find out someone's strengths, you'll know how they can help you, in turn, to reach your goals. People are more likely to help you if you can help them.

Reciprocity is powerful and makes the connection genuine. Identifying someone's goals and skills will usually take more than one short conversation. This is why maintaining a relationship is so integral to the process of connecting. At the end of the day, helping others is one of the most important things you can do in life, and it can also enrich your environment and social circle.

Keeping in touch with people has never been so convenient. With online resources such as facebook, LinkedIn, Twitter, and many others, you can connect with people with ease. Always carry a small note pad and something to write with in the event people don't have a business card (most smart phones will let you takes notes too). Locating the person on social media would be the most efficient method. After collecting peoples' information at a networking event, I look them up on Facebook or LinkedIn and send them a personal message. If they can't be located on social media, I'll send them an email.

In the message, I let the person know that it was a pleasure meeting him or her, and I recap our conversation. If I feel like there is something I need from them sooner rather than later, and/or something they may need from me, I'll invite them to lunch or a cup of coffee. I'll also ask to meet again if I was not able to determine their strength and/or goals during our initial meeting. Be cautious not to let online connecting completely take the place of a good old-fashioned face-to-face meeting.

Let me give you an example of how to make a connection. Recently I met a gentleman at a social function who had a background in marketing. It turned out that we had attended the same college. Below is the follow up message I sent to him.

Sample Message:

Hi John,

It was a pleasure meeting you at the business networking event yesterday. It's always nice bumping into a UNCG alumnus. Your idea of starting a marketing firm was intriguing. I would appreciate the opportunity to learn more about your idea maybe over a cup of coffee. I also wanted to learn how I might be able to assist you with your business. Let me know what your schedule looks like for the next couple of weeks. Look forward to hearing from you soon.

Regards,

Dauv Evans

When you connect with people, they essentially become potential advocates for your goals and vice versa. The people you connect with have areas of expertise, knowledge, access, privilege, funds, and other resources that you may not have access to. When you connect with these people, you have an opportunity to access their resources. How much and how often that access is available is dependent on the dynamics of that specific relationship.

Barry was the type of person who would always know someone who could help. If I needed a job, Barry knew someone. If I needed help with editing my dissertation, Barry knew someone. If I needed quality lawn care service, Barry knew someone. Barry knew someone for just about every need I had. It's no wonder how Barry has achieved the level of success he has to this day.

Reaching goals can be a whole lot easier when you have a team behind you. That reminds me of the old Verizon commercials with the entire network behind the Verizon man.

Knowing that you have a host of people who can help you in one form or another can be reassuring. Remember, each person you meet is an untapped opportunity. When connecting with others, you'll notice how your social circle will begin to grow. You will acquire more friends and meaningful acquaintances on your journey to success.

Hopefully, you now see the benefit of the aforementioned practices. You want to be able to notice opportunities more frequently. Before you begin to notice opportunities, though, you'll need to train your brain to know what it's looking for. Make sure you do more of the things you are passionate about on a weekly basis. Make it a point to meet someone new each time you're out. These practices will increase your ability to notice opportunities.

Opportunities are all around us, and these techniques can help you get better at noticing them. What good is an opportunity if you don't do anything with it? If you purchased a state lottery ticket and later discovered it was a winning lottery ticket, would you throw it in the trash? Of course not; you would make your way to the state lottery ASAP and make them aware of this opportunity in your hand. In other words, an opportunity is only as valuable as the results it yields.

Inhale Opportunities: tailoring your mindset and actions so that you can identify and position yourself amidst opportunities.

Chapter 4

Exhaling Results

"When you do the common things in life in an uncommon way, you will command the attention of the world." ~ *George Washington Carver*

Let's assume you're now the master at noticing opportunities. You know what you want in life. Everywhere you go, you notice organizations, social groups, programs, and people that can help you get what you want. Now what? Noticing opportunities doesn't do you any good if you don't take action. This can be the most challenging part of "breathing success" for several reasons. Sometimes people don't take action because they don't know what the next step is or because they cannot summon the energy or discipline. And sometimes people are just afraid to take any action. When you think about it, ignorance, laziness, and fear can keep you from exhaling results.

Think about our breathing analogy: how productive would you be tomorrow if you inhaled first thing in the morning and held your breath, never exhaling for the rest of the day? You'd pass out before you even had a chance to brush your teeth. Now that your goal is established and you've identified some potential opportunities for getting closer to your goal, let's talk about how to reach for actual results. This chapter will discuss the importance of making those opportunities work for you once you've identified them.

You Can Finally Exhale Now That it's Over

Years ago, I worked for Alltel as a service representative. Even though I met some great people and learned a lot, I wasn't at peace there. I conducted online job searches every day during my lunch hour, looking for other career opportunities. One day I was contacted by University of Phoenix to interview for a job as an enrollment advisor. I was excited because I was passionate about higher education, and I thought this opportunity would get my foot in the door.

Prior to the interview, I was instructed to bring a copy of my résumé and to be prepared to introduce myself. When I got to the interview, there was a room of about 20 people. The hiring manager stood up and introduced himself and told us a little about the position. He then asked everyone to get up and introduce themselves one at a time while attempting to convince him and the rest of the panel why they would be the best fit for the position.

The room was full of extroverts, so one by one, job candidates jumped at the opportunity to present to the group. Everyone else seemed so prepared, as if they'd rehearsed their presentation. I was not prepared to present, and after watching the other candidates, I felt even more intimidated. I remained in my seat strategizing the best way to quickly introduce myself and convince the panel that I would be the best candidate for the job.

I waited the entire time until I was the last candidate left, which I felt made me stick out even more. Depending on how I performed, that could help or hinder me. I slowly walked up to the front, turned around to face everyone, and said... I wish I could tell you what I said, but the experience is a blur. All I remember is pointing to a poster of some graduates dressed in their regalia and hearing some laughter from the other candidates. I can't even recall how long I was up there talking.

I do remember a distinct sinking feeling as I was sitting back down finally able to exhale. I knew I had blown an opportunity, which upset me even more given how seldom I came across job opportunities. The hiring manager thanked us all for our time and informed us of one final step to be considered for the next round of interviews.

The job candidates were required to call the hiring manager's cell phone no later than 8am the next morning and leave a voice message demonstrating how we would respond to a potential student interested in going to school.

I went home that night with no intention of calling that number. I figured there was no point in calling since I made the mistake of winging my presentation and therefore blew a job opportunity. The next morning I got up to get ready for work, and before I walked out the door, a single thought ran through my head: "You can't expect others to believe in you if you don't believe in yourself."

I wanted to ignore that thought so that I could make my way to work, but I figured there couldn't be any harm in leaving the message. I jotted down a few lines on a scrap piece of paper and recited it on the hiring manager's answering service.

Somehow, I made it to the second round of interviews, but I did not receive an offer for one of the two available enrollment advisor positions. My second interview did however lead to a third for another, for which I received an offer.

Follow Through

Before I elaborate on the importance of follow through, let me first make a quick disclaimer. I am in no way, shape, or form a basketball player. With that said, anyone who's ever played or watched the game of basketball will understand there is a basic technique to shooting a basketball. Some of the basics include keeping your eye on the basketball goal, paying attention to your stance, and holding the ball properly. The last step is your follow-through. The follow-through is the proper positioning of your arm, wrist, and fingers after you shoot the ball. You hold that position until you see the end result of your attempted shot.

In both basketball and other endeavors, you'll want to keep your eye on the goal so that all of your actions are purposeful. Your stance and grip on the ball affect the spin trajectory of the ball. This is similar to the way the people you connect with and the activities you participate in affect the trajectory of your life.

The follow-through brings all the elements together. If you were in the process of shooting the ball, keeping your eye on the goal, your stance and grip on the ball would be meaningless without shooting the ball. In life, follow-through means attending to the measureable results of your attempts to reach your life's goal.

Keeping your eye on the goal and setting yourself up for success doesn't matter if you don't follow through. It's very easy to become passive and allow the opportunities to pass you by. I've already covered the importance of pursing your passion and indulging in activities that pique your interest in order to identify opportunities. Now let's talk about how you can measure your follow-through in terms of milestones.

Miles of Milestones

Milestones were originally made of granite or marble and used by the Roman Empire. They were typically placed along the side of roads to reassure travelers they were on the right path. Milestones can be just as beneficial in helping you reach your goals. Adding milestones is the next piece needed to complete your breathing pattern. When looking at your vision board and reflecting on your goals, you'll begin to formulate a plan on how to reach those goals. For each one of those goals, you'll want to set a series of milestones. Milestones help you qualify the amount of progress you're making toward your goal. You'll want even more detail than you used to create your goal statement. Here are a few tips for creating milestones.

Creating Milestones:

- Create your goal statement.

- Clearly outline action items for each milestone in sequential order.

- Create milestones for the steps that are not self-explanatory.

- Your milestones should be time-specific.

- Include the resource(s) that can assist you with each milestone.

Let's return to our goal statement example of starting an online retail clothing store by December 1, 2015. First, you'll want to create milestones that outline the necessary progress. If the idea of an online clothing store is still in its infancy, the first step might be to research how to create a business plan. Remember you can include as many milestones as you want. Some people may need more specific milestones, starting with passing all of the courses for that year or semester.

As a rule of thumb, make milestones for all steps in the process that are not self-explanatory. Using the online retail clothing store example, I used creating a business plan by May 30, 2014, as the sample milestone. Listing each section of the business plan would be too detailed, but simply stating "start a business" as the milestone is too vague. In the end, milestones are a crucial part of your breathing pattern.

Similar to your goal statements, you'll want to be time-specific with your milestones. Each of your milestones will serve as a chronological marker, indicating how much closer you are to achieving your goal. Adding resource is the last piece needed to complete your breathing pattern. You'll want to indicate who can assist you with each milestone and what resources are at your disposal.

Listing the resources can be a helpful step, especially to all the procrastinators out there - you know who you are. I'm talking to the readers who started reading this book a year after purchasing it.

In any case, adding the resource to the milestones makes each milestone more doable. Think about how many times you put something off because you're not quite sure how to get it done or whom to ask. By adding details to your milestones, you make the pursuit of them more seamless. The example on the next page illustrates what this might look like if we continued the goal of starting a business.

Example Breathing Pattern:

Goal: My online retail clothing business will be fully operational and registered by December 1, 2015.

Milestone: Create business plan by May 30, 2014.

Resources:

1. John Johnson (Business Professor): He can review my business plan and provide feedback. Contact him no later than March 1, 2014.

2. Read the book: *How to Start Your Business* by February 1, 2014.

This milestone outlines the next step in reaching your goal, and the resource provides a starting point once it's time to work on this milestone. Adhering to the dates ensures the completion of each milestone in a timely manner.

More than likely, you'll have quite a few milestones, and you may not remember all of the details. Looking at the breathing pattern above, you can imagine how much easier it would be to complete it now that you know what to do, when to do it, who can help, and what resources you have. Let's look at another example.

Example Breathing Pattern:

Goal: I will vacation in Barbados for a week by August 30, 2014.

Milestone: Research the most cost-effective way of to travel to Barbados by November 1, 2013.

Resources:

1. Mother: She might be able to recommend a travel website to me.

2. Ask coworker Mike about his experience traveling to Barbados.

The online business example above illustrates how adding detail to your milestone removes the guess-work from the task. Don't be intimidated by the dates on your goals or milestones. These dates can be adjusted as you progress through your plan. Life happens, and more than likely there will be a few detours along the way. It's helpful to look ahead in case you need to make changes to subsequent dates or resources.

I assure you that it's much easier to make changes to a well laid out plan than to make changes to those undefined ideas you had in your head. Take just a few minutes and try writing a practice milestone on page 89. Be sure to list individuals who can assist you and resources that are at your disposal.

Now that you have constructed this sound plan, you'll want to revisit your plan at least once a day. You can use the breathing pattern templates starting on page 90. You don't have to study the entire plan every day; just take a look at the milestone you're currently working on and maybe take a peek at the next milestone. You can post the plan on your bathroom mirror, refrigerator, or a notebook. It's easy to see the plan if you post it someplace you frequent. Hang up the plan in a couple of places if possible; just make sure that any changes you make are made to all the copies.

Now for my favorite milestone tip: *celebrate* the little victories. It's important to reward yourself as you get closer and closer to your goal. Think of something you enjoy, but seldom take the time to do.

Whenever I completed a subsection or two of my dissertation, I would go to the movies or hang out with my friends for a few hours. It's so important to acknowledge these milestones. It can re-energize you and remind you that you are that much closer to your goal.

You may not think that completing a milestone is a big deal, but I'm willing to bet you know at least one person who still hasn't taken just one step toward completing his or her goal. I'll remind you that taking steps to reach your goal is a reward in of itself.

Even if you don't necessarily enjoy a specific milestone, you know it'll lead you to reaching your goal. Not to mention how motivating it can be to make progress. Your celebration is just a bonus. You should be doing something you enjoy.

Earlier I commented on how important follow-through is. Remember, follow-through is attending to the measureable results from your attempts to reach your goal. Your milestones are the guides you'll use to measure your progress. They will serve as a gauge and keep you honest if you're following through and making use of your opportunities. The corresponding resources will remove some of the guess work with how to approach each milestone.

Your goal, milestone, and resource create a breathing pattern which dictates your path to your goal. Now that we've completed the breathing process, it's important to acknowledge the potential challenges that lie ahead. These are the elements in life that make us hold our breath and stifle progress.

Exhale Results: **In life,** attending to the measureable results of your attempts to reach your life's goal.

Chapter 5

Avoiding Foul Air - The Elements that Make Us Hold Our Breath

"It is best to avoid the beginnings of evil." ~ *Henry David Thoreau*

I'm sure you're aware that you will be confronted with obstacles when attempting to accomplish anything in life; that's probably why you're reading this book. Either that, or you just brought this book because you thought Spencer Johnson's *Who Moved My Cheese* was a cookbook. Obstacles are a constant in life, and we can't stop pursuing our goals just because the task has become challenging. We wouldn't do that with breathing, and neither should we do it with pursuing success.

I used to pass by a meat processing plant on the way to a volunteering opportunity. Every time I drove that way, I would automatically hold my breath until I passed the plant. Similarly, my mother has the habit of automatically holding her breath when talking to someone with bad breath. We humans have a visceral reaction to foul air; it prompts us to stop breathing. In the same way, we might be inclined to stop breathing opportunities, so to speak, when we feel that there are no good opportunities around us. We might pause to reflect on our situation, but end up inhaling the negative influences that stifle progress. Next, we'll discuss the common negative influences that inhibit us from breathing.

El Baño

My fear of foreign language classes started in high school when I was enrolled in a Spanish course. My grades were particularly low in this class. Unfortunately, the teacher was not as supportive as I would have liked. Almost every day, the other students would jokingly suggest that I withdraw from the course. During my short time in class, the only word I learned in Spanish, aside from *hola* and ADIÓS, was *el baño*, which means "bathroom." I couldn't even say "I need to go to the bathroom" in Spanish. My ostensible trips to use the bathroom were my opportunities to ditch class because I had no idea what was going on. I had never ditched class before then, but the idea of learning a foreign language was, well, foreign to me.

Imagine sitting in class totally oblivious to the conversation everyone is having around you. The students in class would turn to a page in the textbook, and I would sit there unaware that we had been told to do so or which page we were supposed to turn to. Sometimes students would get out of their seats to participate in an activity, and I would be sitting in my seat wondering what was going on. The most embarrassing situations occurred when the teacher called on me to answer a question. I always had the same answer: "el baño." I tolerated the course as much as I could for about a month before I withdrew from it.

I eventually attended Wake Tech and then transferred to UNC Greensboro, but the years of negative feedback I had received from high school teachers always stuck with me. My high school Spanish class experience left a particularly indelible mark. In college, I lacked confidence in my academic abilities and would second-guess my school-work. In my first year at UNCG, the school had just instituted a new policy that required all Bachelor of Arts students to complete 12 hours (four semesters) of a foreign language; this policy applied to me, as a history major. When I heard this news, my first thought was to go back to Wake Tech and get an Associate's degree. Then someone told me that learning French was easier than learning Spanish, so I enrolled in French for the fall semester of my junior year.

On the first day of class, the professor asked us students who had taken French before, and about half the class raised their hands. He then asked who had taken Spanish in the past; the other half of the class raised their hands. He asked who here took some other foreign language and about two or three people raised their hands. Lastly, he asked who here had not taken a foreign language. I raised my hand feeling confident that at least one other student was going to raise his or her hand in shame with me, but alas: I was the only one.

The professor then told the class that those were the last words he would speak to us in English. From then on, he told us, he would speak only French in class and would expect us to do the same. I thought to myself, "How are you going to speak to us in the language we're trying to learn?" I asked the professor "this is French 101, right?" He replied in French "*Oui.*" I quickly replied "what?" He then began saying some other stuff that I suspect was important, but I can't tell you what it was because it was in French. Needless to say I was lost from then on.

It was like *déjà vu* (look at me breaking out the French), with all the D's and F's I started earning on my assignments. I was off to an inauspicious start, and my chances of passing my first of four French courses appeared dubious at best. On my first French exam, I earned an F, and the professor wrote a note in French on the top right corner of the exam. I stayed after class and asked the professor, "What does this note say on my exam?" He replied, "It says 'please see me after class.'" He proceeded to tell me that he was concerned with my grade in his course and that he recommended I withdraw from the course and return next semester after some tutoring.

I returned to my dorm room feeling frustrated and defeated. Not only was I on the path to failing the course, but also, even the professor was advising that I discontinue the course. All kinds of negative thoughts filled my head. I thought about dropping the course, but that wouldn't solve my problem. I still needed twelve semester hours of a foreign language to graduate. This was a major setback in my collegiate career. Now let's take a closer look at my situation and see if the negative influences operating on me at the time sound familiar to you.

Fear of Failure

It doesn't make much sense to set out to reach for a goal expecting to fail; you only pursue a goal that you expect you can attain. People generally don't bother to try if they expect to fail. Failure scares us for many reasons. When we fail, we feel like we have wasted our time and resources. Failure can make us feel inadequate, or like we don't deserve to reach the goal we are attempting to reach. It can be frustrating to not get what you want. Plus, failure can be downright embarrassing. It makes you fear how people around you will perceive you. Now, who wants to experience all of that? In my experience with foreign language study, my fear of failure might have prevented me from graduating from college.

Fear of failing is normal. We have discussed how you can change your mindset in order to become more creative in identifying opportunities; well, dealing with fear of failure is no different. We have only failed when we have stopped attempting. If you attempted to open a door unaware that it was locked, you might assume you didn't try hard enough the first time and immediately attempt to open the door again.

After trying a few times and realizing the door is locked, you might knock on the door or call someone to let you in. You might go so far as to peek through the window to see if someone is inside. If you really wanted to enter, you would become creative when trying to get through that door. You wouldn't just walk away after one attempt, would you? Once you get inside, it doesn't really matter how many attempts it took you, does it? Once you're inside, the experience of trying to get inside is behind you. Try applying this perspective to your pursuit of success. Success is on the other side of that door, so keep attempting to open it until you get inside.

Negativity Bias

It is extremely difficult to identify opportunities if your mindset is not conditioned to do so. The best practices for identifying opportunities will not be effective if you are hampered by a negativity bias. Negativity bias is a psychological phenomenon in which the mind dwells on unpleasant past experiences instead of positive past experiences. We've all had our share of negative experiences, but if we all let negativity get in our way, no one would reach their goals. In my situation, my negativity bias stemmed from the unpleasant experience in my high school Spanish class.

This negative memory carried over to my French class in college, creating a mental handicap. The experience of being the only student with no prior experience with speaking a foreign language and the inability to comprehend the professor's French lecture altered my mindset each time I stepped into that classroom.

You have probably heard people say "stay positive and good things will happen," or something along those lines. I know that when people used to tell me that, I assumed they were selling me an empty promise. Well, you can believe that promise, and here's why: The negativity bias trains your brain to focus on only the potential unfavorable outcomes, thereby allowing the potential positive outcomes to go unnoticed.

Conversely, your brain is more alert to favorable outcomes when you're expecting good things to happen or are in a positive frame of mind. You've got to get into a positive mindset. There are many ways to do this, but the simplest way is to go on a sort of scavenger hunt for at least one potentially positive outcome. That is, program your brain to find the positive in a situation. The opportunity found in fresher air is better for you anyway.

I have a good friend who, when faced with taking a risk, always imagines the worst possible outcome. For example this friend and I were returning from a road trip from Atlanta, Georgia to Raleigh, North Carolina and he took every opportunity to find the negative in every situation.

At some point in the trip we got a little turned around and I suggested we pull over and ask someone for directions. His response was "let's not, they might turn out to be violent people and hurt us." Later in the trip, we were driving behind a slow truck, so I suggested he pass it. His response was "not now, the driver might try to merge while I'm trying to pass him and kill us." My friend was able to instantly find the most horrific outcomes in every situation which prevented him from doing even the smallest things. We do this all the time, especially with the more challenging tasks.

Before he could devalue the positive statement I just made, I challenged him to focus on at least one potential positive outcome. Now that his brain is searching for an upside, he'll notice anything remotely positive. This is a clever way to use the RAS to your advantage. For example, if we stop to ask for directions we just might get back on the right path. Or if we pass this truck we might get to our destination sooner than later. The next time you go into work thinking that it's going to be a bad day, correct yourself and come up with one potential positive outcome that you can unconsciously search for. After all, success itself is more accessible when you're in a positive frame of mind.

Negative Nellie

We all know at least one Negative Nellie, one of the proverbial haters of the world. (My apologies to any readers named Nellie.) These are the people that have their negativity bias on autopilot and they're always looking for passengers. This may apply to a relative, friend, or coworker in your life. The negativity doesn't always have to be overt.

In either case, whether the negativity you're around is explicit or implicit, that negative energy may become a nuisance or even begin to alter your mindset for the worse. It's often hard to avoid the Negative Nellie in your life, especially if there's more than one. My high school Spanish teacher and classmates were my Negative Nellies.

Here's how you handle your negative Nellies and haters: Don't! Feeding into their negativity only sucks you into their way of viewing the world. I'm sure you're familiar with the axiom "misery loves company." This holds true with Nellies, and they'll leave the light on for you—trust me. The last thing you want to do is be sidetracked by others.

Don't be surprised if their negative comments persists even after you've reached a major milestone or goal; Nellies need a hobby. Let their negativity be the fuel that energizes you and exponentially intensifies your desire to succeed.

Setbacks

While you are pursing your goals, there will more than likely be some setbacks. Setbacks can be particularly devastating when you've accumulated a significant amount of momentum; they can also be unpredictable, time-consuming, and costly. For example, maybe you're saving money to start your own business or to pay for school, and then you're suddenly confronted with an expensive medical emergency or loss of employment which quells your progress. For me, the low marks I received in French class felt like major setbacks when they led my professor to recommend that I withdraw from the class.

Remember this: setbacks are only as significant as your breathing patterns allows them to be. The sounder your breathing pattern, which is your goal-planning, the more insignificant the setbacks will seem to you. When you're driving home from work and there's a road block closing off the only route you are familiar with, this can present a significant problem. You would probably need a significant amount of time to find an alternate route home.

Now let's use the same scenario, but this time you familiarized yourself with the two alternate routes ahead of time just in case one or two of them were unavailable. How much of a problem is the initial roadblock now? This is where sound breathing patterns comes into play.

Using the resources you have delineated under each of your goal milestones can help you save time and effort. The more resources you have to devote to each milestone, the more likely you will be completing that milestone. Having a plan also allows you to make adjustments as your sense of the future changes. If you have no plan, on the other hand, any adjustments you make are merely guesses you make with your fingers crossed, so to speak. Success is rarely achieved on one's own. Now let's find out how I did in that French course.

El Baño, **continued**

After contemplating the remarks that my French professor made on my exam, I decided not to withdraw from the course. I wanted to graduate with my cohort, and I didn't want one class to get in the way of that goal. That same day, I created my goal, to pass my French course with at least a B-, and wrote out the milestones leading up to that goal. I visited the Student Resource Center the next day and requested a French tutor. I also created flashcards that were more comprehensive than my previous set I had made before. I wrote entire sentences in French on the flashcards, instead of just a word, and I studied these twice a day.

The most significant resource was my French professor, who I visited every Monday, Wednesday, and Friday during his office hours to discuss that day's lesson. We went over the homework assignments and reviewed my flashcards. We also reviewed the lists I compiled of every French word I didn't understand in class each day. I was pretty much the class stenographer in the beginning. Over time, my questions for the French professor decreased, and my class participation increased. More importantly, my grades improved. I earned a B in French that semester. I can't help but think how I've come a long way from *el baño*.

The challenges that can potentially hinder us from reaching our goals are all around us. It's easy to surrender to life's obstacles, but there's reward in persevering. Understanding the complexity of challenges and how they can be attacked gives you a strategic advantage when setting goals. There are opportunities to be found in life's challenges, but the secret is to be persistent in following your plan for reaching your goals.

Chapter 6

Breathing Easy

"Success is just a breath away." ~ *Dauv Evans, Ph.D.*

Now that you've read the steps required to attaining success, you should make sure you're practicing these steps often. Ideally, you want to get the point where you are breathing success every day without even having to consciously think about it. This takes practice and dedication, but it doesn't have to be as difficult as you might think. Incorporating some common practices into your daily routine can have a tremendous impact on the way you identify and act on opportunities.

The process of attaining success is difficult, but knowing what to reach for and how to reach it should not be a secret. In this chapter, we will revisit some of the main concepts in the previous chapters and add another layer.

Holding My Breath, Continued

In Chapter One, I shared my experience with being laid off and subsequently rediscovering my idea of success. Well, a few months after I was laid off, I finally completed my Ph.D., although this unfortunately had little effect on my job search. By then, I was used to sending dozens of copies of my résumé into what felt like a black hole. I started brainstorming other, more unexpected ways to use my newly obtained degree, and eventually my thoughts turned to the speaking/consulting business that I wanted to start.

I began seeing my situation as an opportunity to start fresh with a new approach to my career. In the past, my lack of time had been one of the biggest challenges to starting my own business, but now, time was something I had more than enough of.

My next move became clear when my wife received a promising career opportunity back in Raleigh, NC, and we started discussing our impending relocation. We decided that I would stay at home fulltime with our then four-month-old son. Lack of time was suddenly an obstacle once more.

While I was at home with our son, I had a lot of time to reevaluate my situation. As I learned this new role of stay-at-home father, I got to know my son on another level. I changed more diapers, made his formula, rocked him to sleep, and took walks in the mall with him. Slowly but surely, I began to embrace my new role. I also gained a greater appreciation for what my wife had done when I was working fulltime and she was at home with our son.

I started to recognize the priceless opportunities I gained by spending more time with my son, opportunities to watch my son develop every day. I realized how much I had missed while I was at work. This experience changed the way I perceived my career. Ultimately, my wife and I agreed that we would both build careers that would afford us significant time to spend with our family. This goal planted the seed for my next opportunity.

Once we were in Raleigh, I began volunteering and attended networking events from time to time. One particular networking event that I found on meetup.com incorporated wine and socializing, and featured two great speakers. At the event, I had the pleasure of running into one of my fellow Toastmaster club members.

After catching up, she told me that the gentleman who ran the networking group was also a professional speaker. She encouraged me to visit my old Toastmasters club and do a speech, and even think about taking a shot at becoming a professional speaker. I was initially hesitant, thinking I had no idea what I should speak about. I hit on the idea of speaking about the life changes I had experienced over the previous year or so.

A couple of weeks later, I did the speech, and the experience was exhilarating. I had almost forgotten how much I love public speaking. After talking it over with my wife, we decided that it would be best for me to pursue my speaking/consulting business fulltime. I wrote out a few goals which were as follows:

My Goals

1) Starting December 1, 2012 spend at least 20 hours a week of uninterrupted fun time with my family.

2) Start my own speaking and consulting business by January 1, 2013.

3) Publish a book by December 31, 2013.

Since then, I have worked diligently to reach those goals and celebrated every milestone with my family. There have been challenges, setbacks, and tough decisions to make.

For example, I had to use a significant portion of my saving in order to start my business. When I started my business, there were moments it felt like my business existed only in my head. I turned down job offers that might have compromised one or more of my goals. Some of you may be thinking "Dauv are you nuts, taking from your savings and turning down job offers."

The sacrifice has been great, but so was the reward. I wake up every day doing something I enjoy that also affords me plenty of time to spend with my family. Getting to this point was no easy task, though. I have made "thinking and living success" a part of my daily routine. Here's how you can do the same.

Breathe the Air Outside

Many people fall into a strict routine and end up avoiding other people all day long. People go to work and come straight back home at the end of the day. You might make a quick stop at a local grocery store or to pay a bill, but other than that you avoid people. Opportunity is not going to force itself upon you, just as air doesn't force itself into your lungs. It is crucial that you deviate from your routine and socialize with others.

Twice a week, you need go somewhere other than work and the grocery store. Socialize outside of work at volunteering events, church gatherings, networking events, or even zoomba classes. One of the weekly events should be a regularly scheduled event, and the other should change up every week. Step out and breathe the air outside of your house; you never know what you might find.

Own Your Breath

Earlier in the book, we discussed how opportunity is as ubiquitous as air. Once you recognize this, the next step is to embrace your situation, no matter how unappealing it is. That is to say, recognize that unfavorable situations, when handled properly, can be a gateway to something great.

Some people become so frustrated with their current situation it blinds them to the opportunities that are currently accessible to them. You might take for granted the opportunities that are in the air. Your situation can possibly be the catalyst that propels you to where you want to be.

Most of us have been involved in situations that make us feel unfortunate. No one likes to be in an unfavorable place in life, but that is a bridge most of us have to cross eventually. You might be stuck in a dead-end job, a meaningless relationship, or a significant amount of debt.

People have a tendency to mentally, physically, or emotionally shut down in the midst of an unfavorable situation. Even though your situation may not be favorable, you still have a responsibility to see it to the end. I completely understand how challenging this can be sometimes. Using your strength(s) can turn a difficult situation to your advantage.

I learned a lot during my tenure as Operations Supervisor, but I was nowhere close to being content with my career at that time. My passion was (and is) for higher education and public speaking, but the Operations Supervisor position required many nonacademic tasks that did not interest me in the least, such as event planning, generating reports, and inventory management. Nothing reminded me of my disinterest more than my weekly one-on-one meetings with my manager. The meetings were ostensibly opportunities for me to receive feedback on my job performance, but I usually left the meetings feeling frustrated and mentally drained. This was not my manager's fault; I simply did not embrace my situation as much as I could have. Instead of mentally withdrawing from my job, I increasingly took advantage of opportunities to participate in duties that interested me.

At one point, our campus was in the process of organizing an open house for one of our newer locations. Of course, my team was responsible for putting it together. I loathed event planning, but I wanted to ensure that my team delivered high quality results nonetheless. There were several speakers lined up for the event, but one of the speakers dropped out the day of the event. I was asked by my manager the morning of the open house if I wanted to present in one of the speaker's stead that evening.

I jumped at the opportunity right away. I familiarized myself with the PowerPoint presentation and made some minor adjustments, all in the course of a few hours. That night, I delivered a presentation on résumé and interview tips. I thought that my presentation was average, but I did thoroughly enjoy giving it.

The next day, some of the participants from the previous night emailed my coworkers with compliments on my presentation. My manager brought the compliments to my attention during our next one-on-one. The positive feedback from the participants energized me. It was a clear indication to me that this was what I need to be doing. Even though I was not ideally suited to the position of Operations Supervisor, being in that role opened up opportunities for me to explore what I like to do.

By embracing my unfavorable situation, I was afforded an opportunity that brought me closer to my career goals. The same can be true for you. When you are on the right path, you'll feel an energized sense of satisfaction. Embrace your situation, even if it's momentarily unfavorable, because it is uniquely yours. Just realize that the rewards stemming from these situations are uniquely yours as well.

This same principle applies to your personal life as well. I mentioned how challenging it was for me to transition to being a stay-at-home father. Once I embraced my new role, though, I was able to find unexpected opportunities specific to my new role; for example, I found the time to start my own business and, most importantly, time to spend with my new family. You can find an opportunity in any situation, but paradoxically, challenging situations usually contain the most opportunities.

Breathe While You're Speaking

At a conference I attended some years ago, I first heard that public speaking is the number one fear in the world. This blew me away. Not because I like public speaking, but because I could think of a myriad of things to be more fearful of, like snakes, spiders, flying, rejection, and clowns, just to name a few.

In any case, if you want to take *connecting with a purpose* to the next level, you should consider public speaking. I think people underestimate the power and influence of having a platform from which to speak. The ability to be able to effectively communicate to a group of people can be a powerful tool.

You do not need to be the world's greatest orator to be successful, but being an effective communicator is necessary. More than likely the audience is not going to maul you while you're speaking. That only happened to me once and that involved a group of teenagers and my advocating for raising the legal drinking age - big mistake.

Effectively speaking to an audience is beneficial for many reasons. It is an efficient way to start to connect with others. This can be especially helpful to those who find it difficult to start conversations at networking or social events. If you are at an event, you might have to tell your story over and over again just to meet a few people. You also have to strike up a conversation with them.

Now imagine you just gave a talk on a topic you're familiar with at a networking or social event and everyone heard what you had to say. When you become a competent speaker, more often than not attendees will come up to you wanting to congratulate, thank, or praise you for your talk.

Also, everyone heard your message, so they already have an icebreaker to meet you. Another benefit to public speaking is conveying your strengths and goals. You will remember this was one of the main reasons for connecting. A platform can be used to implicitly communicate your strengths and goals to everyone listing. This gives attendees a specific reason to come talk to you, to help you, and/or get your help. How many times have you had a specific reason to talk to a speaker after hearing him or her give a talk? Even if the individual's intent is just to congratulate or thank you, that meeting can be a potential opportunity.

Public speaking is an impressive talent. To give a compelling, polish speech in front of a crowd is akin to writing a book or earning an advanced degree. Once people are aware of your talent and expertise, they want to get to know you. By showcasing yourself, you are creating an environment that is more conducive to opportunities finding you. Here are three tips to help you develop as a public speaker.

1) **Be a Perfectionist:** It would be wise to work on your public speaking ability. Regardless of your current comfort level with public speaking, you can join one of the organizations that is geared toward public speaking. There you can hone your general speaking ability or practice a specific speech in a non-intimidating environment. Visit Toastmaster, an organization that is located in many cities throughout the world, or a similar organizations. Also, you might simply video-record yourself so that you can more easily recognize your own areas for improvement.

2) **Be Personal:** Draw on personal stories while developing your talk. These are easier to write and memorize; they also let the audience know something about you. This may not apply if you are the mc or moderator for an event.

3) **Be Real:** Make sure your speech is authentic, true, and about a subject in which you have a genuine interest. Audience members can sense whether you are being real with them.

4) **Be Strategic:** Make sure that the venues where you speak are interested in your message. This will ensure you do not waste any time and will maximize the effectiveness of your talk.

Don't worry about being the best. Learning to speak to a large audience is about learning a new level of communication, gaining self-confidence, and learning more about yourself.

I have personally witnessed some of my fellow toastmasters undergo a transformation from being terrified to speak in front of a small audience to becoming a competent speaker. I understand this can be a challenging task for some, but if you can overcome the initial trepidation, you will be much more effective with communication. I have had opportunities to speak in many different venues. Public speaking has afforded me job opportunities, leadership opportunities, networking opportunities, and much more. I cannot speak highly enough about public speaking. Once when I spoke at an event, an audience member approached me afterward and asked whether I had published a book that was available for purchase.

This person had never heard of me or met me before, but because of one fifteen-minute talk, she wanted to spend money to read more of what I had to say. (Now, if I can just hunt her down to let her know this book has been published.) Just remember, you can certainly find an opportunity by talking to one person, but you can create a plethora of opportunities by talking to a crowd.

It's Like Yoga Class

Many networking and other social groups are out there, but maybe you have not found one that works for you. In Chapter Three, we discussed the importance of attending groups and social functions, but an even more powerful technique for pursuing opportunities is to organize your own group.

Organizing events and groups can be a great way to meet new people with similar interests. Your first thought might be, "That sounds like too much work." Of course there will be some work involved, but the reward can potentially make it worth your while. Here are some reasons you might want to consider starting your own group. Let us imagine that you would like to start your own group for, say, healthcare professionals, or maybe bike enthusiasts. First, you want to ensure that there is an interest in your area for your group. You may know people at work, church, or other social circles who have similar interests as you. Doing research, both on the Internet and through social media, is another good way to scan your community's interest level. If the interest is there, you will want to create the meaning of your group or networking event. Here are just a few parameters you should consider.

Checklist for Forming a Group

1) What is the purpose of your group?

2) What is your role in the group, other than organizer?

3) Whom do you expect/want to attend the event(s), and why would they come?

4) What activities will take place at the event(s) (speakers, music, food, games, networking, etc.)?

5) Where will the event(s) be held?

6) On what time/dates will you meet, and how often will meetings be held?

7) What other roles need to be filled in order for the event(s) to work?

8) How will you communicate to potential and new participants about group/event updates?

9) What is the maximum number of participants you want at the event(s)?

10) Will the event(s) cost you any money, and will you want to charge cover fee/dues?

11) Will your target members be able and willing to pay the necessary fees/dues?

Once you are able to answer the questions, you will have a solid foundation on which to form your group. Depending upon the nature of the event you want to host, you'll want to find a suitable venue. Sometimes churches and restaurants can be accommodating. There are also art galleries, libraries, and other businesses that may rent out their spaces after hours for a small fee; sometimes venues will waive the fee because having a group there is good advertising.

As to your own advertising, getting the word out can also be more effective if you work smarter not harder. After you have culled the details for your event, use the Internet to spread the word. Facebook, LinkedIn, Twitter, Instagram, Eventbrite, or even a simple website with a link to email you can be a great way to get attention for your event.

There is also good old-fashioned word of mouth. You might find that there are others who are interested in your event who want to help; you do not always have to organize it yourself. Remember, work smarter, not harder; this often means delegating some tasks to competent assistants.

Let us suppose that you are an out-of-work healthcare professional. How advantageous would it be for you to host a networking event for other healthcare professionals? Maybe you could organize the event with other professionals in the field whom you know.

To give another example, for people in an exclusive relationship, planning a social event as a couple can be rewarding. The couple will not only have the experience of planning the event together, but could also meet other interesting couples to connect with. When you create a group or event, you are using a common interest to gather people into your social or professional circle.

People all around the world gather to practice yoga in groups.

This ancient practice advocates focusing on breathing as the foundation for finding peace. You can organize events for people to practice breathing...success. You can *find* an opportunity by attending one event, but you can *create* opportunities by organizing an event. Breathing success can be a joint venture.

Breathing Success Assessment Results

Hopefully you completed the Breathing Success Assessment at the beginning of the book. Not to worry; this assessment is merely a rough indicator of how you currently define success.

45 You're breathing success!

44 - 36 You need to take some deep breaths

< 36 You're holding your breath

A score of 45 indicates that your definition of success is consistent with the definition outlined in this book. You currently have the potential to breathe success. A score between 44 - 36 indicates that you have the potential to breathe success, but that there are societal constraints upon your definition of success. A score of 36 or below indicates a definition of success that is out of sync with the definition used in this book, a definition that is heavily influenced by a desire for the lifestyle associated with high socioeconomic status.

Regardless of where you fall on the scale, you have the opportunity to define or redefine success for yourself. This book simply offers a definition that can be adapted to your life.

Breathe Easy: Bring it all together

Have your views of success changed at all? Do you *feel* successful in life? What do you need to do in order to become or remain successful in life? Hopefully, this book has offered you a new perspective on success and some specific ideas for how to pursue it on a daily basis.

Each of us has the power to make our situation in life work for us or against us. Your perspective on life is going to determine whether your situation is an opportunity or a threat.

You might have noticed the many opportunities I was able to take advantage of because I indulged in my passion of public speaking and presenting when I had the chance. My passion afforded me opportunities even when I was unaware of the beneficial situation unfolding right before me. Regardless of where I was in life, my passion added purpose to my life. When I eventually became aware of the opportunities available to me through my passion, I began to gravitate toward situations where I felt at peace.

I believe that you ought to choose to see your situation as an opportunity. I am successful in life not because of how much money I make or what I do for a living. Rather, I am successful because I spend my days pursuing meaningful goals that make my conversations, interactions, thoughts, intentions, and obligations satisfying. At the end of the day it brings me peace to know I am filling my life with activities, conversations, and people that truly matter to me.

How much time do you spend each day on meaningless pursuits? I decided to start each day with the right mindset to be successful. I wanted to make success as effortless as Martin Luther King Jr., Warren Buffett, and the other people I saw in those documentaries. Don't waste any more precious time. Start your day off by saying this mantra every morning.

Mantra:

I inhale opportunities

I exhale results

I breathe success

I've been saying this mantra every morning for years. When I say "I inhale opportunities" I inhale. I then exhale after I say "I exhale results." Saying this mantra gets me in the right frame of mind to remember what's important to me and what I need to do to maintain my state of peace. You should try it. Build the life you want, and you won't regret it. Choose to inhale opportunities. Choose to exhale results. Remember, success is just a breath away!

Success = Inhale Opportunities + Exhale Results

Practice Breathing Pattern

Write a breathing pattern, including relevant milestones and corresponding resources on the next page. Make sure that your goal meets the SMART criteria.

SMART Goals

- **S**pecific: Target precisely what you want.

- **M**easureable: Determine the indicator of progress.

- **A**ttainable: Be sure that this goal can be achieved, given the available resources.

- **R**elevant: Decide that the goal is worth the effort of pursuing.

- **T**imely: Determine the timeframe in which the goal should be achieved.

Practice Breathing Pattern

Goal:

1st **Milestone:**

    Resources:

2nd **Milestone:**

    Resources:

3rd **Milestone:**

    Resources:

Use the subsequent pages to write out your three breathing patterns. You can reuse your practice breathing pattern if you'd like.

Breathing Pattern One

Goal:

    Milestone:

        Resources:

    Milestone:

        Resources:

    Milestone:

        Resources:

    Milestone:

        Resources:

    Milestone:

Breathing Pattern Two

Goal:

    Milestone:

        Resources:

    Milestone:

        Resources:

    Milestone:

        Resources:

    Milestone:

        Resources:

    Milestone:

Breathing Pattern Three

Goal:

Milestone:

Resources:

Milestone:

Resources:

Milestone:

Resources:

Milestone:

Resources:

Milestone:

About The Author

Dauv Evans, Ph.D., is the Founder and Chief Success Officer (CSO) of Keen Advisors, LLC. Keen Advisors, LLC specializes in personal and professional development for organizations and individuals. Dauv has served others as a professional speaker and consultant sharing his inspirational message with organizations, working professionals, and college students. He wants others to be successful at overcoming the "how" by finding the opportunities in the "now."

His background is in higher education and corporate training. He earned a Ph.D. in Leadership in Higher Education from Capella University. He also holds an MBA from University of Phoenix and a B.A. in History from the University of North Carolina at Greensboro. Along with running his speaking and consulting business, he teaches undergraduate business and U.S. History. Dauv enjoys traveling the country, sharing his story to help others become better at life.

For more resources and booking information please visit www.dauvevans.com

Contact Dauv at devans@dauvevans.com

K | A

Keen Advisors, LLC | Personal & Professional Development

.

Thought Bubble

Thought Bubble

Thought Bubble